Robert

In the expectation of many contents together all fond wishes

GOLF WITH TONY JACKLIN

by

TONY JACKLIN

with

Jack Wood

J. M. DENT & SONS LTD

LONDON

Set by
The Moorgate Typesetting Co. Ltd.
London
Printed in Great Britain by
Morrison & Gibb Ltd.
London and Edinburgh
for
J. M. DENT & SONS LTD.
Aldine House · Bedford Street · London
First published 1969

SBN : 460 03895 8

CONTENTS

INTRODUCTION

My first target in golf was a series of humps some 160 yards down the first fairway at Scunthorpe. I was eleven and using a ladies' three wood. I quickly scaled this first Everest. Scunthorpe is not a fashionable club and hitting a ball for a carry of 160 yards is not exactly a golfing summit. Since then my horizons have broadened. There were those who laughed at me a few years ago, when I said, even before my first win in a British tournament, that I wanted to be the best golfer in the world!

For years we in England, through long season after long season, and repeated failure after failure, had been fed with the idea that the Americans, Australians, and South Africans were invincible. The last Briton to win the Open Championship was Max Faulkner in 1951. I was the son of a lorry driver hard pushed to keep things going at home, and, six

years old, I had no time to dream of a career in golf. It was, in my environment, a game for those who drove more comfortable vehicles than the old man's lorry, and, among the lads with whom I played in the street, unquestionably a game for those with money. Yet here I was in 1966 talking of being the best golfer in the world. If since then I have gone some way to achieving this remarkable but attainable peak in sport, much of the ground-work was done in those early days.

This is an underlying truth which I would like to drive home to young boys reading this who have not yet taken their first steps in the greatest and most rewarding game of all. In the new social structure, it no longer matters what the old man does for a living. The achievements of men like Palmer, Player and Nicklaus have made golf a front-and-back-page sport, and I am surely right in saying that

Palmer has for some years been one of the most publicized and respected figures in world sport.

Every boy with a leaning to games can now realize his golfing ambition, and after the recent developments in my short career I can tell them that life at or near the top in golf is just about the most exciting way of earning a living yet invented. I truly have no idea of what else I would be doing at this moment, because from my early teens I had no other target.

As you may imagine, life for young Tony Jacklin was tough for a long while. I was always a fiercely independent kid, and because I wanted to get together my equipment and earn enough money to be able to pay my way at a humble little club, I took early steps to supplement the pocket money the old man could ill afford. I have read stories of tycoons who made their first acquaintance with money by selling newspapers, and although I am not yet in the tycoon bracket I, too, can look back on wet and often snow-driven mornings humping a huge bag of papers around the streets and up to the steel works of Appleby Frodingham.

I used to stand at the entrance to the factory selling the old *Daily Herald*, the *Express* and the *Mirror* to the men with flat caps and grey faces who earned their living in one of the toughest and (then) certainly least rewarding of industries. They got to know the dark-haired kid with the papers and the hunk of bread and jam in his hand, and day after day let him know that he would be a nutcase to follow them into the steel works. I was maybe thirteen at the time. Having already known the joy of hitting a golf ball past those humps at the first, I decided to give up most other sports and make myself into a golfer who would one day turn professional. I did another job on Saturday mornings for one of those quick-sale traders in Scunthorpe market. My chief role was to hand up the goods to this talkative selling wizard from Leeds, but occasionally he would let me go in for a little selling. Maybe that's why I have never found it difficult to talk in public.

For months when I began in golf I could not break 92, then one day something extraordinary happened to my game and I shot an 84. No further improvement came for six months, but then I broke 80 for the first time and realized that if you try hard enough and play the game to the limits of your own ability and strength, anything is possible.

Soon the rather tubby kid who sold papers in the mornings and sheets and towels in the market on Saturdays began to make a name for himself in local golf. I won the first four club competitions I entered at Scunthorpe, and in my first 'away' tournament at Elsham did the last nine holes in par figures for a 63 net. At thirteen I had played nine holes to a scratch handicap: Things were looking up!

In the Lincolnshire Boys' Championship over my own course, I had an 81 in the first round and then a 66 to break both the professional and amateur records.

I did go into the steel works for a time, at a wage of £3 11s. 3d. a week, and played football for one of the work's teams. I kept pulling muscles and having to miss golf, and it was at this time that I decided that all other sports had to be sacrificed.

From that time golf for me became a year-round sport, and my involvement was complete.

The pro at Holme Hall had a net, so in the back yard I rigged up my own practice net. It consisted of an asbestos sheet, and for balls I used little chunks of rubber cut off a hose. This made a hell of a din, and I am sure the neighbours in strictly working class Holme Street thought I had gone mad.

During school holidays my golfing day usually embraced a full twelve hours. After the paper round I would collect a loaf cut in half with a good whack of butter and jam, and leave home at eight in the morning. Mother and Father wouldn't see me again until eight in the evening.

When my father, Arthur, congratulated me after I had won £8,300 in the Jacksonville Open, he said happily: 'Well done son, you deserve it'. Maybe he was thinking back to those days of paper rounds, the asbestos sheet, balls made of old bits of hose pipe, chunks of bread and jam, and the long days at the golf club where I would help the green-keeper in the morning, practise in the afternoon, and in the summer months have a game with the older members in the evenings.

Like most boys in the street, I liked the occasional cigarette, but Woodbines were 9d for five and well out of reach of a pocket emptied in pursuit of a burning ambition. But I still had my cigarettes by buying fag papers and collecting tab ends from the ash trays at the club when the steward wasn't looking. Odd, but now I can afford it, I smoke about three a day and often give them up for months.

For my work on the course, the green-keeper used to give me a couple of balls most days, and I used to find a few myself. I suppose in some ways I was a bit of a horror, always on the lookout for some way of making a shilling or two so that I could acquire the tools of the trade which has made me reasonably rich at twenty-four and, I hope, secured a future for my family.

Those days had their lighter and more embarrassing moments. While the big boys were in the bar one Sunday morning, I dis-turbed the customary pint sinking and got a ticking off from the Club Captain. I was practising chipping near the bar window and mis-hit what was meant to be a delicate little shot—an attempt to cut one up. The ball went straight through the bar window and on to the billiard table. I was tough even in those days, but the things old Jack Webster said to me then had me in tears. Soon I was in the English and British Boys' sides, but lack of money meant that I had no chance of playing in the fashion-able amateur events. About this time began a struggle with my parents, who told me that I was lucky to have a regular job in the steel-works; on no account would I be allowed to become an assistant pro.

However, Sam Kennedy, a local character, who often helped me, called at the club and told me that Australian Bill Shankland had advertised for an assistant at Potters Bar. I applied for the job. My father came with me for the interview in November 1961, and I was offered £6 a week plus 50% of teaching and playing fees. This seemed like a fortune, and I could also save most of it.

A Mrs Baker said that she would take me in for a week until I got settled into permanent digs. This turned out to be one of those lucky breaks: she is still one of my closest friends and still puts my wife and me up when we are back in London. I used to pay her £3 15s a week, and after a while bought a suit from an uncle for a fiver. The Jacklin boy had not exactly made it, but at least he looked the part. Bill Shankland turned out to be the hardest task-master imaginable. He pointed out that although I had been something of a little tin god around Scunthorpe, where I had been Boys' Champion four times and beaten everyone out of sight, I had now joined the big league and was absolutely no different from anybody else. I needed discipline and under Shanko I certainly got it. After three months I won the Middlesex Assistants' title, and was on my way in this new sphere. The Dunlop people considered that I had a certain amount of promise, and after winning that Assistants' title I took possession of my first-ever set of new clubs. There were times when it was heartbreaking, with long hours spent practising under the keen eye of Bill Shankland. Looking back I realize that he taught me more about the golf swing than anyone else. But he often criticized my work around the shop and, I thought, made life a little tougher than it might have been. But Bill had always been a tough egg both in Rugby League and golf, and maybe his aim was to produce not just a good golfer but a fighter. For three years I played golf and practised, helped in the shop and spent my evenings in my digs or at the cinema.

The main line north used to run past the Club. I longed so often to nip over the fence and on to the train home, so that I could be back with my folks, that I am still wondering why, on at least one occasion, I did not do just that. Kids always have dreams, and a frequent one of mine was of pulling into the car park with a car at least as big as the boss's. Maybe I wanted to run before I could walk and take too large a slice of life's good things before I had earned them.

Then in 1963 the sun began to shine on the kid over whom the dark clouds had rolled for so long. I played in the Coxmoor Tournament and made the last day. My partner was Eric Lester: I realized just how far I had to go before I could call myself a tournament golfer. The same year I also made the last day in my first Open Championship, the one in which Bob Charles beat Phil Rodgers in a play-off at Royal Lytham and St Annes. I finished twenty-ninth.

The Potters Bar members were thrilled, and told me that they would pay for me to play in tournaments for the rest of the season.

The following year I decided to go on tour full-time, and felt that it was unfair to the boss to continue drawing a wage from him. He saw it this way too. I continued to be affiliated to the Club, but without a retainer. I was on my own.

In the early part of the winter I kept myself by playing with members for side stakes. Johnny Rubens, who in July 1968 was to organize a wonderful dinner for me in London, offered me £200 to help me tour South Africa. Dunlop gave me another £200, and with most of my savings I was able to make my first trip outside Britain.

To call this trip a disaster would be an under-statement. I found the greens virtually unread-able; when I came back I had exactly £35 in prize money and a beautiful sun-tan, but unless you are a male model the bronzed look is no sort of currency. There is not much you can do with a tan when you're skint. This was my financial set-up when I went to Pleasant Valley, Boston, and won 1,000 dollars in the Carling Championship by finishing thirty-fourth. I flew straight back, rang the P.G.A. and asked for a late teeing-off time, drove to Hartsbourne and shot 74 after a 4,000-mile journey and no sleep. I qualified for the last two rounds with a birdie three at the last hole, then shot two 68s and won a play-off with David Butler and Sean Hunt for the Assistants' title.

The peak was round the corner. I made a good start the following season (1966) and was third three times in a row in the Penfold, the Agfa, and the Martini. But that first win among the seniors was still eluding me. Still, the money was coming in; and the day before I married Vivien I won the Blaxnit in Belfast and was picked to play for England in the Canada Cup in Tokyo. The big wide world was beginning to open up, and all the effort and the heart-break suddenly seemed worthwhile. I went back to South Africa, and this time won a tournament at Kimberley and £1,000.

In 1967 Neil Coles, the British star who hates flying, did not want to travel to the Masters. I took his place. Peter Butler had done well at Augusta the previous year, and on the way over in the plane to that most famous of courses and celebrated of championships, I kept telling myself that what Butler could do I too could do.

This was without question the break-through. At one stage during the second round of the world's most colourful tournament I led the field, and at the half-way stage I was second. I then shot 74 and 77. A number of friends among the writers made excuses for me and praised my boldness in going for everything. To be perfectly honest, the pressure got me in the heat and splendour of Augusta, and I cracked. In spite of this I felt that my temperament was suited to the hard grind of the American circuit, and that my game was suited to their courses. Maybe it was reaction, but I played badly and putted worse when I came back to Britain until the Pringle at Royal Lytham, where four years earlier I had played in my first Open. Suddenly my swing got back into its groove, the putts began to drop, and I won my first major tournament on the eve of my departure for the Canadian Open.

My experience in Augusta and the general liking for the American and Canadian way of life convinced me that my future lay across the Atlantic, and it was then that I decided to play most of my golf on that side of the Atlantic. There are more tournaments, the prize money is bigger, and winning is more difficult. To play there is an essential part in the development of any young golfer. You just cannot make the top by staying in Britain, where golf too often has the atmosphere of a charming but hardly exacting garden party.

The crowd reaction is in strange contrast to that of the huge galleries across the Atlantic. Maybe golf crowds are too reserved in Britain. I sometimes felt that they only clapped to keep their hands warm.

I was eleventh in the Canadian Open and won $4,000. In September a hole in one at the sixteenth at Royal St Georges clinched the first prize of £1,250 in the Dunlop Masters. The same year I went to Houston for the Ryder Cup, then on to Las Vegas, the Caribbean and Hawaii.

Just before the Masters, I agreed to play under the Mark McCormack banner, and under him moved into 1968; a year in which both the cash and the fame reached an unforgettable peak. Gaining confidence every week in my first assault on the big American prizes, I moved nearer to the jackpot, and in April I landed the first prize of $20,000 in the Jacksonville Open. Henry Cotton had won a two-day event in the United States in 1947, but I was the first modern-day Briton to win a full-scale tournament there.

The rest of the year, although profitable beyond my wildest dreams, was something of an anti-climax. When I came back to Britain for the Open Championship at Carnoustie, I was given star treatment. Immediately after Jacksonville, the Jacklin boy was front-page news, and an awful lot of people expected me to follow up with victory in the Open. An eight at the comparatively easy seventh hole ruined my chances, but my last tournament appearance in England took me out of a wonderful year on a high note.

Against Gary Player in the semi-final of the Piccadilly Match Play Championship at Wentworth, I had six birdies in the last nine holes to square the match. I wanted to go on that dull Friday evening, for I felt that I could beat Gary in the sudden-death play-off.

Unfortunately, the organizers abandoned play, and when we eventually got down to settling things on the Sunday morning, I lost at the first hole, where Gary holed a nine-foot putt for a four, and harangued the crowd for what he considered to be their bad sportsmanship.

The year ended with a trip to Australia for Viv and myself; but we couldn't wait to get back to Lincolnshire and the house we had bought, and which we will use as a base. It is our first home, and perhaps for the first time in my life, I have real security.

PUTTING

The late George Duncan, Open Champion in 1921 and perhaps the quickest stroke-maker in the history of golf, was criticized shortly after winning the Open, when in an exhibition match in Leeds he missed a putt of a couple of feet.

'Fancy an Open Champion missing a little one like that', said one of the greenside crowd in those far-off days. George, often as hasty in temper as he was in playing his shots, turned on his critic and said, 'Aye, mon, yon hole is four and a quarter inches across, and the whole damned world is around it.'

You will not need me to tell you that the whole point of golf is to get a ball with a diameter of no more than 1·68 inches into a target 4¼ inches across. Huge fortunes depend weekly on the ability of the top players to make the vital putts, and with the advance in technique that we have seen during recent years in other departments of the game, putting has become the vital factor in deciding the destination of the mammoth prizes.

The rest of the game is what Tony Lema once described as a cross-country wild goose chase in search of a climax. And to achieve the best results in this decisive stage of the game, there can be no hard-and-fast rule on either how the club is held or the putting stroke made.

In recent years men like Sam Snead and that great English amateur of yesterday, Leonard Crawley, adopted the croquet style, because in putting with the ball and club between their legs they were able to use bifocal vision in lining up the putt and hitting the ball to a target. Early in 1968 golf rulers on both sides of the Atlantic outlawed this croquet style, and a number of golfers nearing the end of their careers decided to quit the game rather than submit to what seems to have been an autocratic ruling.

Step 1.

Step 2.

Step 3.

Step 4.

PUTTING

Step 1. Adopt a comfortable stance; that is, one which suits you best, and line yourself up with eyes directly over the ball.

Step 2. Take the blade away smoothly without any jerkiness and do not lift the putter on the back swing; keep it as low as possible.

Step 3. At the end of the back swing remain calm and at this stage try to feel the weight of the putter in the hands.

Step 4. Keep the hands ahead of the putter as it approaches the ball.

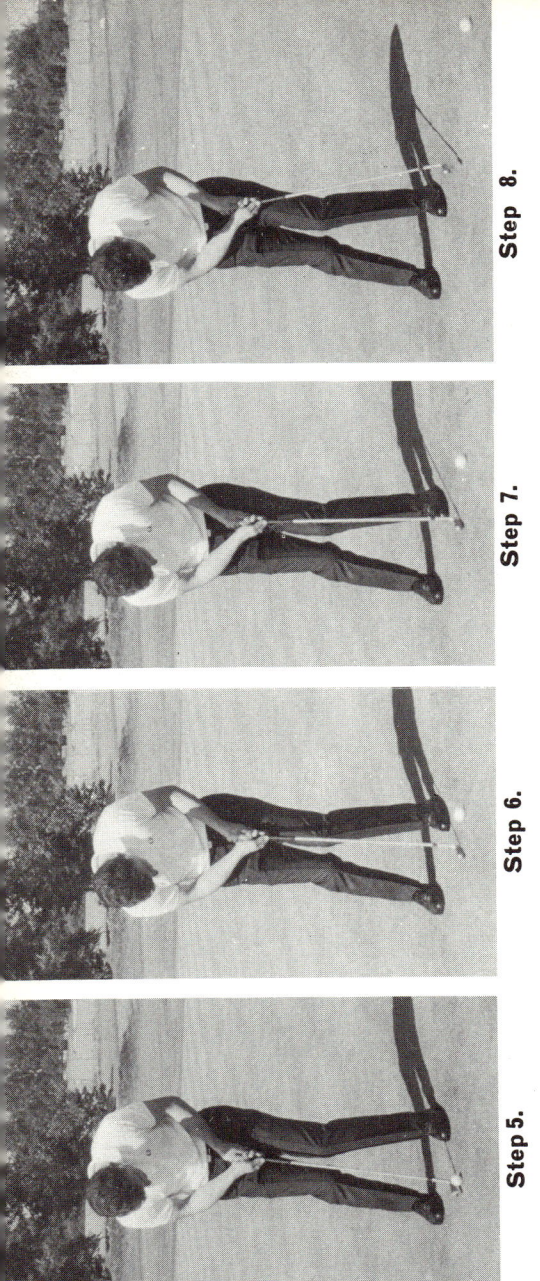

Step 5. **Step 6.** **Step 7.** **Step 8.**

Step 5. On contact keep the body absolutely still.

Step 6. Strike smoothly and still on a low plane, which is maintained at the start of the follow-through.

Step 7. The head has still not moved, the eyes still fixed on the spot where the ball was.

Step 8. The completed smooth follow-through will ensure earlier that you have rolled the ball smoothly away and created top spin.

But back to those of us who prefer to putt in the conventional way. Ben Hogan, among others, declared many years ago that golf consisted of two different games, the first played in the air in making progress from tee to green, and the other in getting the ball into the hole.

In the nineteen-sixties the best putters have almost certainly been Arnold Palmer, Jack Nicklaus, Gary Player and Billy Casper. Yet if you study pictures of them in action, you have four completely different approaches to this vital exercise of holing out.

The first essential is to be comfortable in both the grip you take of the shaft and in the stance you adopt. As I have said, top players differ from one another, but most of them use the reverse overlap: that is the forefinger of the left hand overlapping the little finger of the right. When you have taken a grip of the club the stance is usually slightly closed; that is, the left foot a little in front of the right.

The putting stroke is a question of feel. You will go out on some days and know from the start that the majority of your putts are going to finish either in the hole or very close to it.

I always stand more erect for the longer putts because this gives me a better perspective and a better feel. But Nicklaus drapes his huge frame over the ball for putts of all distances, and when he is in form there is no better putter in the world.

When faced with an uphill putt one must necessarily hit the ball harder, and it follows that with a downhill run to the hole the strength of stroke is less. I usually hit downhill putts off the toe of the putter; that is, away from the sweet spot, so that the ball doesn't come off the blade so quickly.

The one essential in this vital department of the golf game is to keep the body absolutely still throughout the stroke, and to keep the head down long after the ball has left the putter blade. Hogan summed it all up with his 'hit and hark' doctrine. You hit a ball, keep your head down and wait for the noise of the ball rattling into the hole.

In Britain, golf is fortunate in that the grass used on greens has a finer texture than in other parts of the world, and the reading of the grain of the grass is not so important. In South Africa and the Far East a coarser type of grass is used because this stands up better to the heat, and I well remember on my first trip to South Africa how difficult it was to read the grain. Although the greens at the Augusta National Club in Georgia compare well with any in the world, the grain changes with the direction of cutting, and with a long putt the ball appears to fish-tail on its way to the hole.

However, you can usually spot which way the grain is going, and it is a matter of common sense that when you are putting with the grain, the ball needs to be hit less firmly. In a way it is like pushing a boat, in this case a golf ball, up or down stream. Putting is largely a question of experience. You will find out early in the round just how fast the greens are. When they are fast I slacken my grip slightly, thereby adjusting the distance the ball runs without changing the putting stroke. Some people use a putter with a lighter head when the greens are fast, but it is too much to expect the club golfer to go in for this sort of thing.

It will be obvious that on greens heavy because of dew or well-soaked grass, putts must be struck harder, and on those dried out by the sun or wind, the stroke will need to be less firm.

In lining up the ball and the hole, many people pick a spot some way along the line of the putt at which they aim, but in my view this is complicating a very difficult business even more, and I prefer to get in my mind a picture of the path the ball is going to take on its way to the hole. Judging the borrow of a putt is a matter of experience, and caddies familiar with the strange twists of greens on a particular course often give one an alarming line to the hole. But they know what they are talking about, and this is why a caddy of experience can be of great value when you are playing a strange course.

The average golfer cannot afford a caddy, and you will get a good idea of the borrow you need to take by looking at the putt from the other side of the hole. To judge accurately the contour of the green between the ball and the hole, it is best to take up a mid-way position and get down on your haunches.

With all putts, keep the putter low. This ensures the correct strike with a certain amount

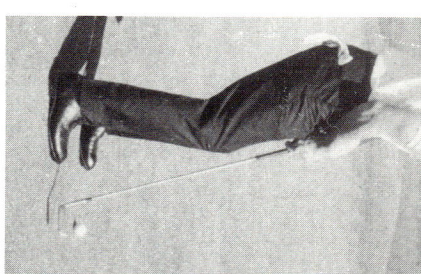
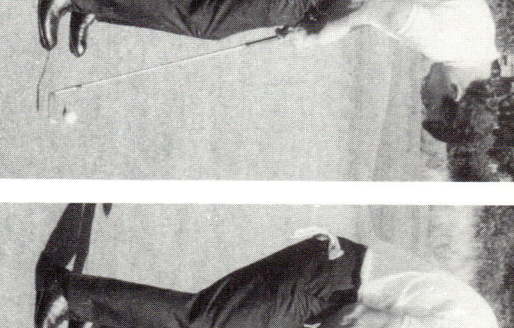

Step 1.   Step 2.   Step 3.   Step 4.

PUTTING

Step 1. Square, comfortable stance, eye over ball, blade square to hole.

Step 2. Takeaway is smooth, slow, keeping putter face square and low.

Step 3. Head absolutely still as you move through ball with smooth firm stroke.

Step 4. Head remains still as putter blade follows through on line to hole.

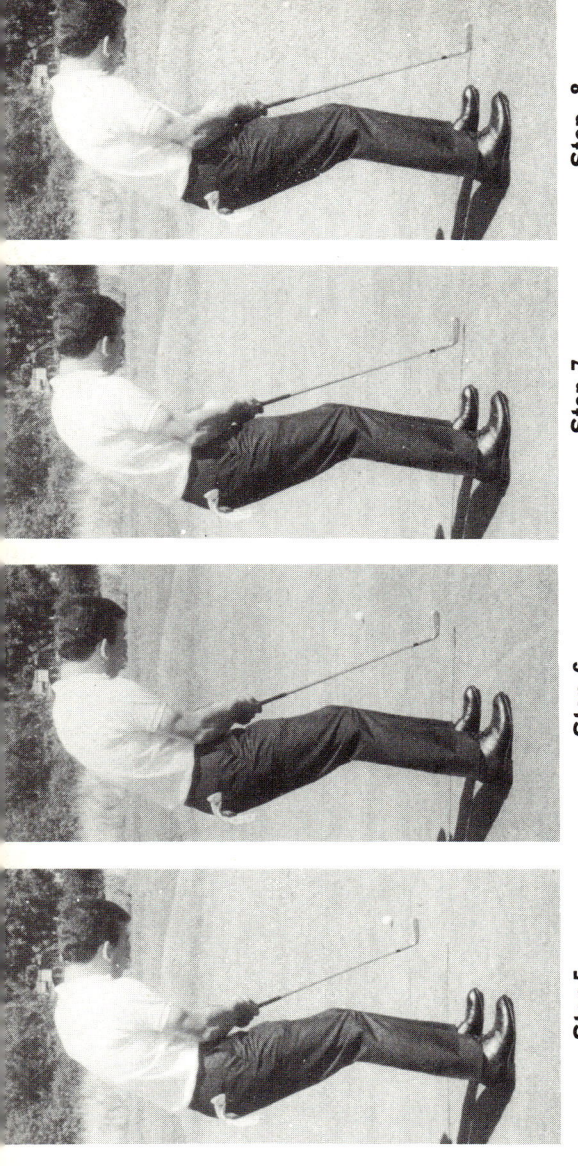

Step 5.   Step 6.   Step 7.   Step 8.

Step 5. Blade leaves its low plane for first time at end of follow-through.

Step 6. As blade recoils, eyes follow progress of ball to hole.

Step 7. With ball nearing hole, blade returns smoothly almost to address position.

Step 8. Throughout movement, body and legs remain still but relaxed.

of top spin, whereas if you take the blade high on the back-swing you will come down on to the ball and give it back spin. Obviously if you can putt well, you will score low. The often-depressing truth in golf is that no matter how far and accurately you hit the tee shots and the second shots, the figure on your card at the end of the hole depends on how well you hit the putts, whether they be tramliners or shorties of two and three feet.

If the par of a course is 72, 36 of those shots will be allocated to putting; that is, two putts per green. Apart from the croquet style used only recently by so many good players, there has been a trend in recent years to reverse the position of the hands completely, with the left hand below the right. Peter Alliss had a long spell using this method, and claimed that he had more feel by leading the stroke with the palm of his left hand pointed along the line.

Remember that unlike most other shots, the putt is essentially made with the hand and forearm, and that it is played with no movement of the body. The wrists are the hinges which control the movement of the shaft, and there-

fore the blade and the club are swung like a pendulum.

Because putting is controlled by the hands and forearm, it is essential to keep them close to the body with the right elbow braced against the right side, so that movement is limited to the hands and wrists.

With right-handers the putt is actually struck with the right hand. In recent years players have tended to rap the ball towards the hole with the right hand, and in doing this the ball is hit with the blade of the club after a back-swing of no more than a foot.

The role of the left hand is that of a leader, taking the blade along the line and bringing the right hand into the hitting position. 'Never up, never in' is an old golf axiom. It stands to reason that the ball has not even a million-to-one chance of dropping if you do not get it to the hole. Yet, because the majority of golfers are scared of running the ball too far past, the great majority of the putts of the millions struck round the world on a Sunday morning finish short of target.

The United States Open Champion of 1968,

Lee Trevino, is one of the best putters in the business, and he has a theory that the dying putt is the one with the greatest chance of success. By this he means that a ball which is pulling up and going for the right or left hand edge of the cup has a much better chance of dropping into the hole than a ball which still has some life left in it. But this ability to judge distance so accurately that the ball dies as it reaches the hole is most difficult to achieve, and for the average player I recommend boldness on the greens. In putting more than in any other department of golf, it is essential to give the ball a chance.

More nonsense is talked about putting, and in action more strange routines practised, than about any other department of the game. The boring five-hour rounds which have become commonplace in the United States are largely due to long-drawn-out rituals on the green. I suppose amateurs have watched the professionals both live and on television taking all day over their putts, and feel that they must do the same. We professionals might appear to spend an indecent time lining things up, but we are, after all, playing for big prizes and any indecision can be disastrous.

When near the hole, think positively and give yourself a chance by hitting the ball firmly. Many golfers exaggerate the effect of "borrow" with these short putts.

Undoubtedly the big prizes have brought a new anxiety into putting. This anxiety is often born of the desire to win a fortune, and should not spread to those who play the game for fun. Golf is a fun game, but it will not be so for you if you become both a mathematician and over-diligent perfectionist on the green.

SHORT APPROACH

SHORT IRON

Step 1. Sit well down over the ball with knees bent and slightly open stance to ensure left hip is cleared in follow-through.

For the amateur with a handicap of ten and more, the short approach from 75 yards or so in is the most vital part of golf. On most holes the low-handicap player can be expected to make the green in two, but in order to give himself a chance of par the ordinary golfer must develop accuracy in his short game. If you can get the ball somewhere near the hole from the often-difficult spots around the green, you will pick up a fair percentage of one-putts and give yourself a chance of scoring well. It is exciting and rewarding to hit a booming drive and those low, raking second shots. But the percentage game is in the area close to the green where power is of little use and accuracy absolutely essential.

The grip remains the same as for all other shots with the irons and woods, but because you do not need the distance given by a long arc, it is essential in these short approach shots to take the hands down the grip. The hands are thus nearer the club face and striking area, and you get a more positive feeling of more control.

For these shots use an open stance. This will give you a better view of the hole and enable you to judge the distance better as you line up your shot.

Before making the shot choose a spot at which to aim: a spot from where, with reasonable luck, the ball will run up close to the hole.

Naturally, if there are obstacles like bunkers, bushes or hillocks between ball and hole, a pitching wedge will be used so that the ball can sail over them before hitting the green.

With the pitching wedge the swing is naturally restricted, but the stroke must still be a positive and crisp one, and the divot taken.

As in all other shots, the follow-through is important. But most club golfers are afraid of following through, because for some reason they feel that to do so will send the ball hurtling beyond the green.

The wedge will give back spin if properly played from an open stance, and the ball's landing point will be alongside or even beyond the hole.

If the terrain is rough or muddy, a pitching wedge is the only club to play.

In Britain many of the runs-in to the pin are fairly clear of trouble, and the green is usually harder than the well-watered putting surfaces found in the United States. The chip with the ball landing some way short of the target often pays a bigger dividend. If there are no obstacles, a chip will often be most profitable. This can be made with clubs varying between the five and seven iron.

The pitch and the chip are soft shots, using a half or three-quarter swing, and because there is a natural desire to see the ball dropping near to or running up to the hole there is a tendency to spring at the ball. This completely destroys timing. In addition, the club head is not swung through, but is thrown at the ball and the inevitable result is that you quit on the shot. The chip shot is, in fact, nothing more than an exaggerated putt with a lofted iron. The

SHORT IRON

Step 2. Smooth, one piece takeaway is essential. Breaking of wrists and body movement laterally must be avoided at all costs.

principles used in each distance and direction are the same as on the green, and by taking the hands down the shaft, often to the bottom of the grip, the necessary control is obtained. One advantage you have in developing accuracy with the chip and the pitch is that the shot can be practised in the corner of the garden or in open land nearby.

With the medium to short irons, that is the five, six, and seven, the carefully played pitch from the open stance will give you top spin and will set the ball running on to the hole. In playing the shot, keep the right elbow well down and comfortably tucked into the side, with the weight resting a fraction towards the left side. The feet will be closer together than for the shots in the longer game, and because a lot of wrist and forearm come into the shot, the rest of the body should be anchored with the knees acting as swivels.

The club is taken straight back from the ball with the palm of the right hand, with the back of the left hand remaining square to the hole throughout. There is little arc in this shot, the club head remaining close to the surface except at the very end of what amounts to a tight little back swing, but remember that the follow-through must be loose and easy and, until you are adept, slightly exaggerated.

Because one is so anxious to see the result of the shot, there is a tendency to dip into it and bring the head up too quickly. This also results from a natural desire to scoop the ball a little when in fact the blade of the club is made to do the job.

Naturally the farther you are from the hole the longer will be the arc of the swing, but the principles are the same: club head close to the ground until just before the finish of the back swing, body still, no attempt to scoop the ball up, and head down.

As with the chip, the wedge is in essence a three-quarter shot, but because of the design of the club, with its heavy flanged sole, it will pop the ball up over the intervening obstacles and down near the target.

Play the ball from just forward of the centre line, and when you want to stop the ball quickly, open the face a little. If you need the high trajectory the club gives but still some run on landing, close the face as with the pitch, get the back of the left hand facing the hole and hit down and through.

For the short punch shot which will negotiate a near hazard, break the wrists almost as soon as you take the club back, keeping the hands well ahead of the club. The club is dropped down and into the ball almost with a chopping motion, but instead of stopping the club you swing through firmly with a positive wrist action. In playing from a grass lie from which the ball will rise quickly, the stance is with the ball nearer to the back foot so that the club face comes into the shot before it reaches the bottom of the swing.

SHORT IRON

Step 3. Head must be absolutely still as the arms force the clubhead back low away from the ball.

OUT OF THE SAND TRAP

The bunker is a much-maligned part of the golf course. The average player has a fear of it quite out of proportion to the problems it sets; indeed many good players prefer to play for the pin from sand than to pitch from grass. Gary Player and Julius Boros are two of the best sand trap players in the world, and in recent years the Asian stars with their deft touch have become absolute wizards with these shots.

First of all the feet go into the trap. Make sure, by shuffling the feet around and then pushing them down into the sand, that you have a solid and comfortable platform for the shot. Once you have, the shot still presents a few problems. The stance must be open and the club taken back more sharply from the ball, which means breaking the wrists sooner.

SAND BLAST

Step 1. Grip and stance are almost identical to that used for fairway pitch shot. But clubface is more open.

SHORT IRON

Step 4. Keeping the clubhead low ensures the wide arc required, but the movement must be easy and in no way forced.

The broad sole on the sand wedge is designed to create a good passage through the sand, and to go with a splashing effect which will get the ball up over the lip of the trap. A good follow-through is absolutely essential to a well-executed bunker shot. A closed club face would dig the club down into the sand and not give that effective splash out which is necessary.

Remember as you weigh up the shot that the more sand you take the less back spin you will get.

With buried lies you will have to use your own judgement, and in these cases, as in playing very bad rough, your first and foremost concern must be recovery from trouble.

Playing from the down slope of a trap is one of the most difficult shots in golf, but again, the takeaway must be steeper than usual and the ball must be got up quickly.

With long shots from the beach remember first that no matter how well you try to anchor yourself, it will be impossible on most occasions to get the same leg action—and therefore the same power—as from the tee and fairway.

SAND BLAST

Step 2. The club must be held above sand and at no time touch either sand or ball. Touching either brings penalty.

SHORT IRON

Step 5. Now the right hip turns away from the ball, but the left heel stays firmly on the ground.

So if normal golf thinking suggests playing from a good lie in a trap to a target far in the distance, club yourself to make up for this inevitable loss of power.

SAND BLAST

Step 3. Now pick a spot in the sand not less than one inch behind ball at which spot clubhead will enter sand at impact.

SHORT IRON

Step 6. The wrists are now fully cocked at top of backswing, but the hands must remain firm on the grip.

32

SAND BLAST

Step 4. The backswing begins with the wrists cocking more quickly than with wedge pitch shot to ensure a more vertical arc and a cut under ball.

SHORT IRON

Step 7. As downswing begins, so the left hip begins to move open and on the line of flight.

SAND BLAST

Step 5. Note that although the arm and knee positions are much the same as for pitch, the left foot remains firm.

SHORT IRON

Step 8. The hips are well ahead as the left hand pulls the clubhead towards the ball, thus achieving the necessary leverage.

SAND BLAST

Step 6. Top of backswing is reached, showing that one must now cut across ball from slightly more open stance.

37

SHORT IRON

Step 9. Although the knees are still flexed, they are sliding forward and pulling the hands into the hitting area.

38

SAND BLAST

Step 7. The bell-pull action is repeated as the left hand draws clubhead down into the hitting area.

39

SHORT IRON

Step 10. As the power is poured in, the head must remain anchored as the right shoulder begins to pass under the chin.

SAND BLAST

Step 8. The wrists now begin to uncock rapidly to apply power required to blast ball out of sand.

41

SHORT IRON

Step 11. The left hip is now moving aside as the knees pull the hands through the ball.

SAND BLAST

Step 9. Sole of sand wedge is about to cut into sand behind ball. It never actually touches ball.

43

SHORT IRON

Step 12. The body remains firm at the moment of impact as the right shoulder passes under (not round) the chin.

SAND BLAST

Step 10. The moment of impact. Once again the right shoulder is coming underneath the chin, and both head and body, although relaxed, are perfectly still.

45

SHORT IRON

Step 13. Hip and head remain down. As the hands pull onwards through the ball, resist a natural temptation to watch the ball rise.

SAND BLAST

Step 11. The sand starts to fly as it is forced against the ball, which therefore rises rapidly.

47

SHORT IRON

Step 14. With the target so near, the tendency is to lift the head and follow the flight because it can be seen throughout and the result of the shot can be crucial.

48

SAND BLAST

Step 12. This is the point at which so many handicap golfers quit on this shot. But it is essential to keep clubhead moving through the ball.

SHORT IRON

Step 15. Note how the arms carry on the follow-through on line of flight—no quitting or scooping.

SAND BLAST

Step 13. Note that the eyes are still on spot you originally picked in the sand.

51

SHORT IRON

Step 16. The relaxed, perfectly balanced finish to the shot, right heel raised, the right shoulder past the chin. **NOW** you can watch the ball.

SAND BLAST

Step 14. Without this follow-through the clubhead will dig too deep into sand, with too-often-seen result that ball stays in trap.

53

DRIVING FROM THE TEE

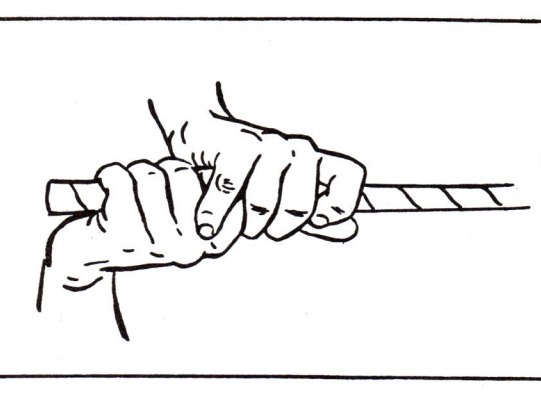

The overlapping grip.

The Grip

The golden rule in gripping the club is that although it is held in the hands, it is actually gripped in the fingers. The fingers provide the most sensitive contact through the shaft to the club head, and when this feel of hitting the ball 'with the fingers' is at its finest, the golf shot will also be to the limit of your ability. There are days when you go out and have no feel. The player who is consistently successful is one whose fingers in fact give this feeling of actually striking the ball. Without this finely defined control of the club, you have no chance of making an effective shot. The placing of the hands is the first step in setting up the action which is known as the golf swing. Place the club head of your driver behind an imaginary ball and allow the shaft to rest across the left hand.

SAND BLAST

Step 15. At last the head begins to come up as the right shoulder has passed the chin.

55

Close the left hand over the grip with the butt of the shaft nestling onto the fleshy part of the hand across the palm from the base of the thumb. At this point feel that the club is being held with the small and second finger of the left hand. The other two fingers—that is, the middle and index fingers—are only supporting the shaft with the thumb resting on it so that the 'V' formed by the thumb and left index finger is pointing towards the right shoulder. We are now gripping the club with two fingers and holding it with the left hand. The points of application of those two fingers are the first of the five pressure points in the golf grip.

Now place the right hand round the shaft so that the left thumb fits nicely into the groove formed by the hollow of the palm and the thumb pad of the right hand. The shaft is now gripped with the thumb and first two fingers of the right hand with the little finger of this hand in the over-lapping position—that is, the Vardon grip—with the little finger on top of the left index finger. You now have a golf grip. It is used by well over 90% of players and will give you the best service. For anyone with small

hands, however, an interlocking grip might be more comfortable; *i.e.* little finger round left index finger.

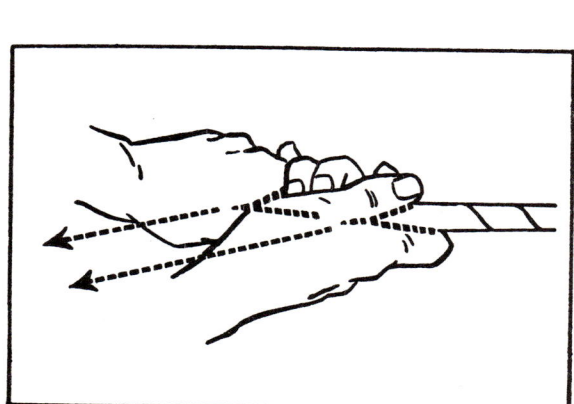

The 'V'.

56

SAND BLAST

Step 16. The right hand has ridden over the left to complete the cut-up shot and you can now see ball.

The Stance

In addressing the ball the weight is settled comfortably on the balls of your feet with the knees slightly flexed. In making the golf swing, the knees are unlocked. If they are rigid at address, the flexibility needed to unlock them will not be there.

The face of the club lies squarely behind the ball, and without any feeling of pushing out, the arms should reach for the ball. From this position, with the ball level with the left heel, a swing can be achieved. The left foot should be turned to an angle of 30° towards the hole. This enables the follow-through to be executed without any unnatural barrier, and this positioning of the left foot round towards the hole is in my view one of the great secrets of the golf game. The feet are spaced at shoulder width for the drive. The key to this vital business of setting yourself up for the drive is a feeling of perfect balance. With the weight distributed properly, you get the feeling that, as you take the club head away from the ball to the top of the back swing down into the hitting area and on for the follow-through, there

is no chance of swinging yourself off your feet. Only experience can bring this feeling at all times.

We are now set to begin the back swing. The first rule, in fact one of golf's golden rules, is to begin the back swing slowly. This will, in the early days, be difficult, particularly under pressure, for having lined up for the shot it is the understandable desire of handicap golfers to get on with it, to get the whole business done with and the ball on its way.

The line from the base of the spine to the head is quite straight and the club head is on its way back: *slowly* on its way back. The left arm takes the club on the beginning of its journey, and later will bring it into the hitting area at a speed which has been accurately computed as in the region of 100 m.p.h.

The right shoulder is slightly lower than the left, and a moment's thought will tell you why. The right hand is lower down the shaft. The head will remain still throughout the back swing, and as the club head speeds up on the way down to the hitting area, it should also stay fixed.

58

The Full Swing

To watch a top class player swing a golf club is one of the most exciting sights in sport. In recent years Sam Snead, Billy Casper and the late Tony Lema have been perhaps the smoothest swingers. With Arnold Palmer and Jack Nicklaus the impression gained has been more one of the application of power than the sweet unforced application of club head to ball. There has always been the perfect mixture of timing and rhythm in Snead's seemingly unhurried method, but because the timing has always been so superb he could always, in his heyday, keep up with the so called power-man. Lema was also as long as most of them and Casper is among the longest iron players in the game. Timing is the thing you have either got or you haven't. Many great sportsmen in other fields have taken to golf with startling ease and might have become first-class players had they spent more time at the game. Men like Ted Dexter, Colin Cowdrey, Sir Len Hutton and Denis Compton could have played well enough to establish themselves in the professional golf game.

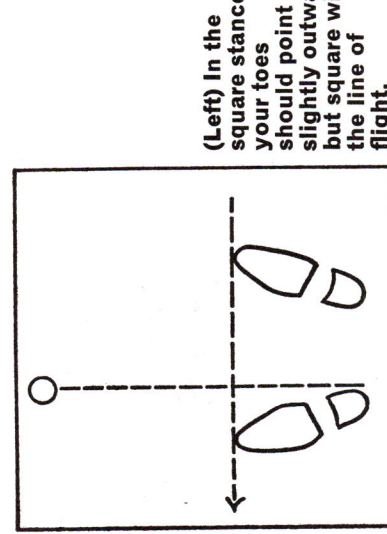

(Left) In the square stance, your toes should point slightly outwards but square with the line of flight.

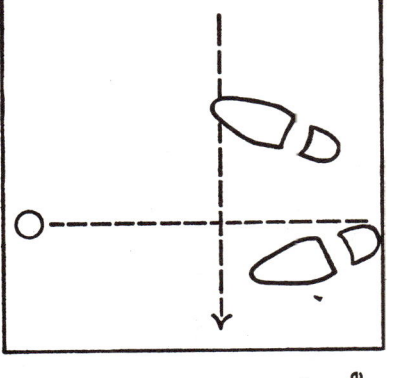

(Right) Your stance is 'opened' by drawing your forward foot back from the line of flight.

Without this strange gift of timing the golf game will inevitably be more difficult to master, and in fact players will probably do so with a manufactured swing, because left to their own feeling of how to use the club, they will make a mess of things. But whether or not you were born with the great natural advantage with which the Lemas and Sneads of this world were blessed, you will make the right sort of golf shot if you follow the general principles of the swing. The whole point of the swing is to bring the club head back to the ball squarely along the line of flight, having produced at the moment of impact the greatest possible club head speed.

So we begin by taking the club back low and on a perfectly straight line for some ten or twelve inches. This is the area in which later you will gain both club head speed and apply direction, the hitting area, and it must be obvious that if this first action is done slowly, the chance of reproducing it in reverse will be greater.

First of all picture the path of the club

throughout the swing. You will get a much better mental view of that path if you take the club back slowly. Most top players begin with a forward press. This is, in effect, a slight pushing of the body against a braced left leg with the hands carried slightly ahead of the ball.

In taking the club head away at the beginning of the swing, it is in effect pushed away from the ball by the left arm and hand. As the club head continues back, the left arm remains extended to the full and the club gets into the horizontal position with the right arm tucked into the body down as far as the right arm will automatically produce a bending of the right arm with the left knee angling in towards the ball, the right leg now taking the shift of weight.

The left shoulder being the extremity of the line formed by the straight left arm and its extension, the club shaft, it will move under the chin, moving the shoulders through 90 degrees.

Poised at the top of the back swing, the coiled spring is ready for release. We now pass into another transference of weight, with the hips leading the way. They will now slide forward and you will be aware of a sensation of dragging the club into the down swing.

The left arm is locked and is in effect drawing the club down along the same path it had taken a fraction of a second earlier in the back swing. As the club head, now travelling very much faster, moves through the swing arc the right arm straightens, and suddenly the most important components become the hands and wrists. It is here that power is developed.

The hips, being already past the square position and opening up to the target, are naturally ahead of the hands. This creates leverage which gives the desired clubhead speed.

Step 1.

Step 2.

Step 3.

Step 4.

SHORT IRON

Step 1. Opening the left foot towards the line of flight aids the follow-through which is to come by giving hip clearance.

Step 2-3. Take the club away smoothly. As the club proceeds on the back swing, keep the

body absolutely still with no lateral movement, and the head as if glued to the shoulders.

Step 4. Make for the shot a good wide arc, but still be completely relaxed, without any strain.

Step 5.

Step 6.

Step 7.

Step 8.

Step 5. The hips turn away from the ball but the left foot remains anchored to the ground.

Step 6. At the top of the back swing the hands must be firm on the club, with particular emphasis on the left hand.

Step 7. The left hip is already moving open and towards the target.

Step 8. Pulling with the left hand into the ball, the hips have moved ahead and are now giving leverage.

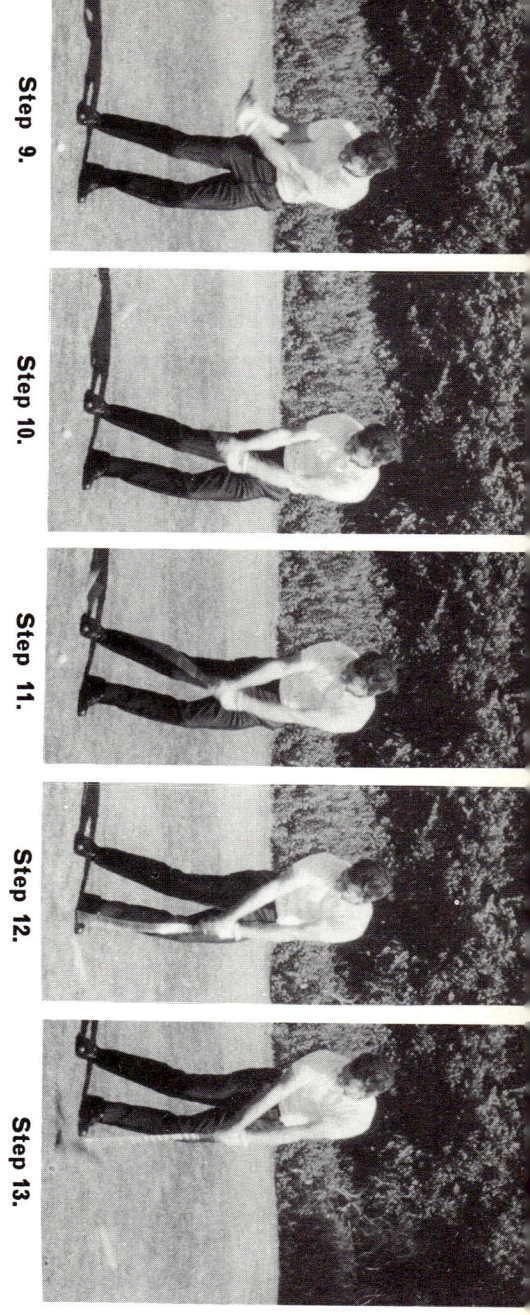

Step 9. **Step 10.** **Step 11.** **Step 12.** **Step 13.**

SHORT IRON

Step 9. The knees are still flexed and the ideal feeling is that of the knees leading the hands into the shot.

Step 10-11. The head is very still and the right shoulder begins to go under the chin.

Step 12-13. There is a very natural desire to see the ball rise on its way to the target, but the hip and head must stay down through the shot with no suggestion of a scooping action.

Step 14.

Step 15.

Step 16.

Step 14. The ball has gone but the head remains still.

Step 15. A good follow-through with the arms: never quit on the shot or try to steer the ball.

Step 16. The right shoulder comes through under the chin, leading into a well-balanced, relaxed finish.

Step 1. Step 2. Step 3. Step 4. Step 5.

THE SAND BLAST

Steps 1-2-3. Club face well open, also stance open at address. Club must be picked up rather sharply (Steps 3-4) and a spot in the sand chosen, about one inch behind the ball, at which the strike will be made.

Step 4. Wrists cocked quicker than on fairway irons for steep takeaway.

Step 5. Right hip moves away, but left heel remains firm.

Step 6.   Step 7.   Step 8.   Step 9.   Step 10.

Step 6. Head anchored at top of backswing.

Step 7. Knees move forward as bell-pull action starts.

Step 8. Wrists uncock quickly to apply blasting power.

Step 9. Head still stationary as right shoulder starts to pass under chin.

Step 10. Clubhead enters sand at spot where you are aiming and watching.

Step 11.

Step 12.

Step 13.

THE SAND BLAST

Step 11. Don't quit now or you will dig too deep.

Step 12. Explosion of sand causes ball to rise steeply.

Step 13. Note firmness of follow-through.

Step 14.

Step 15.

Step 16.

Steps 14-15-16. A good follow-through is absolutely essential. Without this follow-through the club will tend to dig too deep, with a resultant misjudged shot.

The essential in mastering the sand wedge is to practise and practise again. Perhaps more than in any other shot in golf, a feel is necessary when playing from sand. But I emphasize again it is a shot over which one should not have nightmares. Many golfers trudge into the sand with a feeling of impending doom. It is, in effect, one of the more simple shots of the golf game.

Step 1.　　Step 2.　　Step 3.　　Step 4.　　Step 5.

THE DRIVE

Step 1. Ball addressed off the left heel with a firm grip by the left hand. Take the club head back slowly for the first twelve inches, pushing it away from the ball with the extended left arm (Steps 2-3). Create a wide arc but still with no lateral movement (Steps 4 and 5).

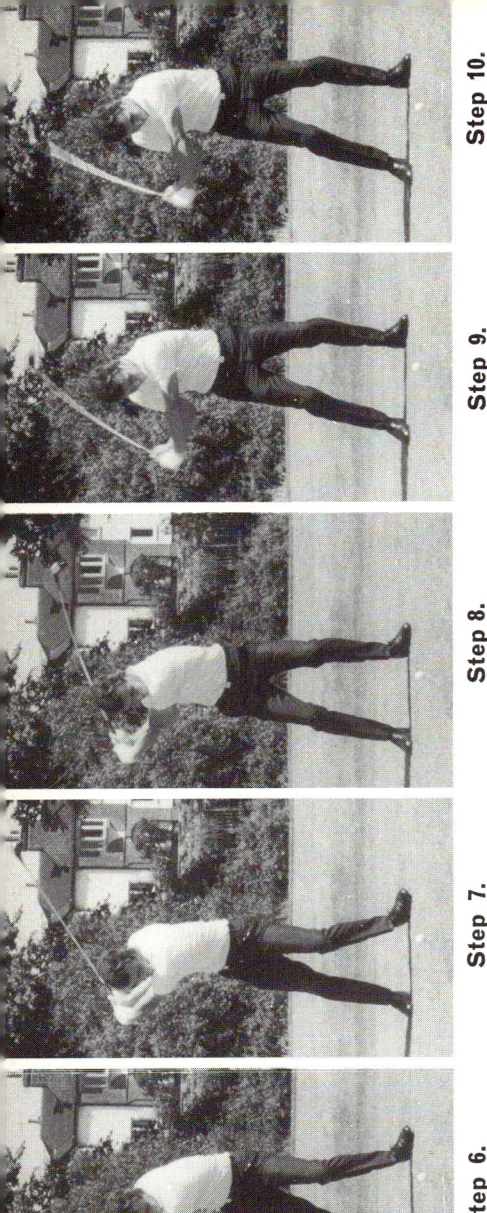

Step 6.   Step 7.   Step 8.   Step 9.   Step 10.

Shoulders will turn through 90° at the top of the back swing with the hips turning through 45° (Steps 6-7-8).

Now the uncoiling begins (Step 9). The left hand pulls the club head down (Step 10) into the hitting area (it is helpful to imagine you are trying to putt the end of the shaft into the ground).

Step 11. Step 12. Step 13. Step 14. Step 15.

THE DRIVE

Steps 11-12-13. As the hands pull down, the left hip leads the down swing.

Steps 14-15. Contact is made with the hips now normal, facing the line of flight. The hands are not far behind, generating power as they pull through without losing balance or momentum. The right hand is now forcing itself against the left and providing the whipping action.

Step 16.

Step 17.

Step 18.

Step 19.

Step 16. The right shoulder moves under the chin and on through (Steps 17-18-19) for a good high finish.

73

Step 20.

Step 21.

Steps 20-21-22. Balance must be maintained at all times, otherwise control and power are lost.

Step 22.

See Flip Sequence of the Drive, starting on page 84.

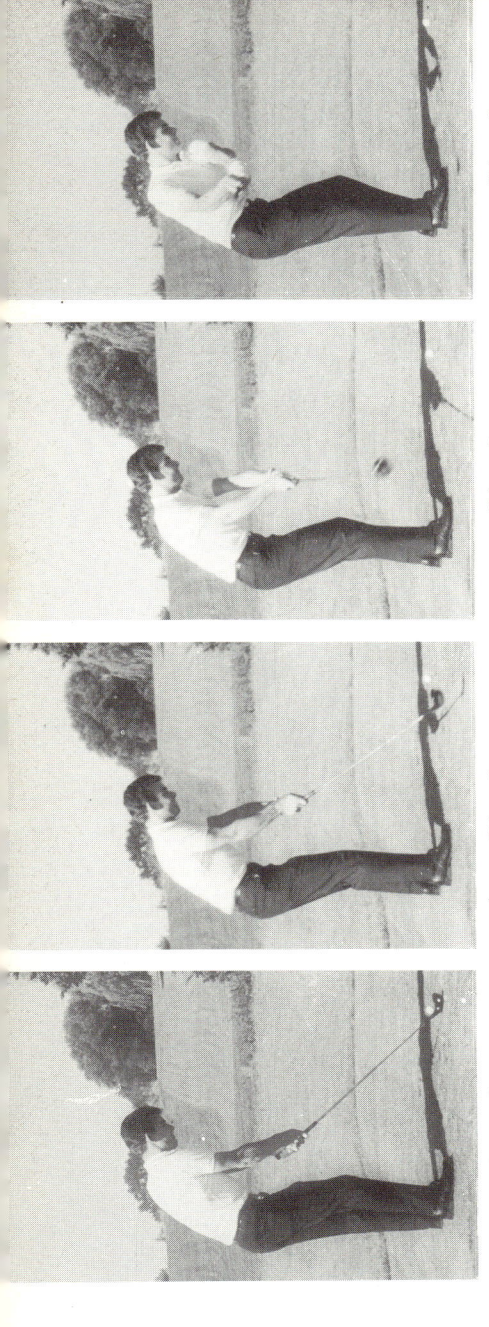

Step 1.

Step 2.

Step 3.

Step 4.

THE DRIVE

Step 1. Knees relaxed, hands and arms firm.

Step 2. Start of one-piece takeaway.

Step 3. Left hand and shaft in straight line.

Step 4. Right hip moves round, as wrists start to cock.

Step 5.

Step 6.

Step 7.

Step 8.

THE DRIVE

Step 5. Left heel lifts fractionally . . .

. . . as top of backswing (Step 6) is reached.

Step 7. The spring starts to uncoil . . .

. . . as left heel slams down again (Step 8).

Step 9.

Step 10.

Step 11.

Step 12.

Step 9. Once again left arm and hand are pulling club down.

Step 10. The weight shifts back to left foot as left foot clears.

Step 11. Right knee and foot push into ball . . .

. . . as hands whip the clubhead through it (Step 12).

Step 13.

Step 14.

Step 15.

Step 16.

THE DRIVE

Step 13. The ball is driven away with left arm fully extended.

. . . well through hitting area (Step 15) . . .

Step 14. The head remains stationary . . .

. . . as right shoulder comes underneath (Step 16).

Step 17. **Step 18.** **Step 19.** **Step 20.**

Step 17. Now the head is forced to lift . . .

. . . but perfect balance is maintained (Step 18).

Step 19. The weight is now almost all on left foot . . .

. . . as the high follow-through is reached (Step 20) with hands still firm on club.

DRIVING PROBLEMS

How to effect the fade and hook

The ball will fade; that is die to the right towards the end of its trajectory, if a slight clockwise spin is imparted. To produce this spin, adopt a slightly open stance, take the club head slightly outside the normal swing line and bring it inside that line. This adjusted swing brings the club head across the ball from right to left and produces the spin we are looking for. To produce a hook, adopt a slightly closed stance. This time take the club head back on the inside of the normal swing arc and outside that arc in the hitting area. This will bring the club head from left to right across the ball and give it the left-handed or anti-clockwise spin which produces a hook.

Curing a slice

To do this, bring the right foot back a little and be sure that you take the club back on the correct swing arc. If necessary, adopt this hooker's stance, and swing until you get rid

of the slice which is so obviously worrying you if you have gone to the length of looking for a cure. The reverse procedure is followed in getting rid of the hook.

Shanking

This is perhaps the most celebrated fault in golf. Many terrible stories are told of people developing a shank, and never being able to rid themselves permanently of the affliction.

The basic cause of the shank is taking the club head away with an open face and lateral sway. The ball is usually hit in a shank with the pipe of the club—that is, the inner extremity of the face—and the result is a disastrous spraying of the ball to the right. Millions of words have been written on the shank and ways of curing it. If you never get it, you forget about it until you are its victim. When you get it, try to overcome it by taking the club back with both hands in one piece to avoid the opening of the club face and to guard against lateral sway.

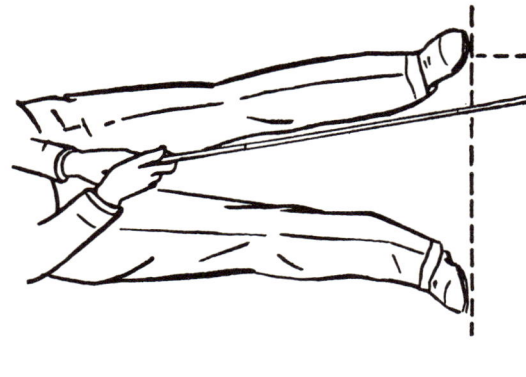

The drive is the only shot with a wood that is a sweep. You want to get top spin, and thus more roll with your drive. The way to do it is to keep your standard swing but play the ball off your left toe and keep your hands back at address.

Hitting versus sweeping

Sweeping the ball is a result of trying to keep the club head going through at a steady pace instead of releasing the club head at the ball on the way into the impact area, thus causing a crack or snap as the ball is struck, instead of the dull *whoosh* of the one-pace sweep shot, which will obviously not send the ball as far.

Topping

This is the main cause of an often embarrassing scuffle of the ball not too far in front of the tee. Topping is always the outcome of jerking up the head and body.

Pulling

A pulled shot is, as the name suggests, one which is yanked rather than hit crisply. It is usually preceded by lateral movement which can often be described as a lurch, and the result is that the ball finishes far to the left of the intended line.

Smothering

The club head has travelled from inside to out and is therefore produced at impact, the face of the club head in a position in which it stifles the ball and never allows it to get airborne. To overcome this, open the stance and make sure that the club is taken back on the correct arc or, in the case of a really bad attack, slightly outside to in.

Tension

The tension of the fingers is, as I have explained, the way to good golf. We all seek to achieve exactly the correct tension at the five pressure points of the grip, but most players would rather do without the mental tension, which in most cases increases with the importance of the occasion.

It is a well-known medical fact that the excitement of the big occasion, the desire to produce performance at peak level, produces an adrenalin flow which gives one greater muscular power and therefore a potentially greater standard of achievement. Jack Nicklaus rates his hitting power as 20 yards stronger when the adrenalin flows, although few experience a 'change' of such proportions. You should bear in mind that in an exciting match your power increases. Most of us suffer from tension when the chips are down and have different ways of overcoming it. I try to breathe more deeply and to do everything a little more slowly. Performance is always improved under tension, and it gives that little extra edge and snap to your game. But being too tense has ruined the victory chances of many. Some players whistle to themselves, others hum a favourite tune. It doesn't matter how you slacken off when tension hits you; just find the way which is personally most effective.

Windy days

The problems faced in high winds obviously vary according to the direction of the wind. Don't fight the wind, use it. With a left-to-right wind, don't try to draw the ball into it, but aim left of line so that direction is achieved and maximum distance gained. There is always a tendency to hurry things in a wind: a tendency to get the shot over as quickly as possible. But when it blows, take more time over setting yourself for the shot and swing a little more slowly.

WOODS FROM THE FAIRWAY

With its slightly shorter shaft and an additional six degrees of loft on the club face, the three wood is the ideal weapon for making war from the fairway, although large numbers of players restrict themselves to a four or even five wood, because they feel that clubs having less loft produce difficulties.

With the ball sitting nicely on the fairway a two wood is often possible, but the three is the one you will use most frequently. Position yourself as with the driver, and in general play the ball as you would from the tee, but because of the face loft you can afford to take the hands down the shaft a little. Give yourself a feeling of more control without sacrificing distance.

Obviously the more difficult the lie the more loft you will need, and a four to five wood will be taken. With varying ground conditions your choice of club will be wider. If the fairway is hard and the ball sitting up perfectly, take the wood which will give you length. The difference between a fully hit drive and a three wood will be around 30 yards and you can

afford to sacrifice this distance in order to get the ball cleanly away from the fairway on the right line. With the four to five wood, position the ball a little farther back from the left heel, and come into the ball just before reaching the bottom of the swing, taking a small amount of grass. With the four to five wood the club is swung a little more on an upright line, with the actual blow a downward one as you squeeze the ball off the turf.

Downhill lie

With the ball on a down-slope the club will come up more steeply at the start of the back swing, and on impact will give the ball the clockwise spin which produces the slice. So, from a downhill lie aim more slightly to the left.

Uphill lie

The club face begins the back swing on an even flatter path than is ideal in relation to the ball, and on impact left hand spin will be imparted. So, compensate for a lie of this type in aiming to the right.

THE DRIVE

Step 1. Stance wide but relaxed . . .

LONG IRONS FROM THE FAIRWAY

With the long irons a really positive grip is even more important than with the woods. Most golfers tend to check more on the various points of the grip when taking a wood because they feel that the club needs more control and power in making the stroke. But a weak, sloppy grip with an iron club is invariably more disastrous, and in playing the long iron never try to reassure yourself by laying the blade back.

Modern golf equipment is designed to do exactly what the makers claim for it, and if you decide to try and hit a green some 200 yards away with a three iron, allow the club face to do what it was made for; don't give it help by laying it back a little on address. If you do this and swing the club absolutely perfectly you will get too much loft.

With long irons the area of the face is much less than on the woods and shorter irons, and you will find in general that the medium woods are much easier to use. Yet in the view of many people, the thrill of hitting a two or three iron really well is unmatchable. Some of my most memorable moments centre on the long iron. The iron is played with a slightly closed stance, and you hit down on to the ball taking the divot after it. And, as with the driver, push the left arm down straight as far as possible with the right elbow in tight. Never crouch over the ball.

THE DRIVE

Step 2. . . . with ball addressed off left heel.

86

LONG IRON

Step 1. Feet are shoulder width apart.

THE DRIVE

Step 3. Clubhead taken back slow and square.

LONG IRON

Step 2. Left foot pointing towards target, ball inside left heel . . .

THE DRIVE

Step 4. Extended left arm creates wide arc.

LONG IRON

Step 3. . . . as clubhead is taken away smoothly.

THE DRIVE

Step 5. No lateral sway as right hip turns away.

92

LONG IRON

Step 4. Wrist movement starts . . .

THE DRIVE

Step 6. Shoulders turn fully as wrists cock.

LONG IRON

Step 5. . . . as right elbow gives way to allow shoulder turn.

THE DRIVE

Step 7. Left heel lifts slightly as . . .

LONG IRON

Step 6. Right hip withdraws as wrists break.

THE DRIVE

Step 8. . . . top of backswing is reached
with hands firm.

LONG IRON

Step 7. Top of backswing is reached . . .

99

THE DRIVE

Step 9. The uncoiling begins with left hand pulling clubhead down.

LONG IRON

Step 8. . . . and the left hip starts the downswing.

THE DRIVE

Step 10. Knees are sliding forward but head remains stationary.

LONG IRON

Step 9. The hands pull downwards . . .

THE DRIVE

Step 11. Left hip is leading now as it begins to turn away.

104

LONG IRON

Step 10. . . . as the weight is transferred to the left foot.

THE DRIVE

Step 12. The weight is transferred to
left foot. . . .

LONG IRON

Step 11. The right elbow is tucked in tight . . .

107

THE DRIVE

Step 13. . . . as the right leg supplies drive.

LONG IRON

Step 12. . . . as the hands move into the hitting area.

THE DRIVE

Step 14. The balance is maintained without loss of momentum.

LONG IRON

Step 13. The clubhead is released through, not at, the ball . . .

THE DRIVE

Step 15. The right hand provides whip-ping action . . .

112

LONG IRON

**Step 14. . . . and again the head remains
perfectly still.**

THE DRIVE

Step 16. . . . while the left hand maintains control.

LONG IRON

Step 15. Extend as far through the ball
as possible . . .

115

THE DRIVE

Step 17. The right shoulder moves under
the chin and . . .

LONG IRON

Step 16. . . . making this a conscious mental and physical effort.

117

THE DRIVE

Step 18. . . . onwards towards the firm follow-through.

LONG IRON

Step 17. This will ensure a full follow-through . . . .

119

THE DRIVE

Step 19. Balance is perfect, and the head still stationary.

LONG IRON

Step 18. . . . with the hands finishing high, as only now will the head begin to come up.

121

THE DRIVE

Step 20. As the right hand rides over left . . .

GETTING ACCURACY
AND THEN POWER

Choosing clubs of the right weight

It has been suggested that the choice of golf clubs should be approached with the same care as the choice of a wife. I suppose it depends on which you intend to spend the most time with: the clubs or the wife. But seriously, this business of getting the right clubs is of great importance.

The characteristics you should look for in clubs depend on a number of factors. Golf is a game of confidence—perhaps more than any other game—and to go into it with clubs that may look good but feel terrible is rather like trying to cook an exotic meal on a single gas ring without herbs and spices.

It helps a little, but only a little, to have good-looking clubs. I have known players order

their woods and grips in their favourite colour because this makes them feel better. I have no quarrel with this, but the look of the club is far less important than the feel.

What do we mean by feel? The aim of the golf swing is to develop maximum clubhead speed in the hitting area. You will have some idea if the club feels right as soon as you place it behind the ball. If it is too long, too heavy, or badly balanced, you will know then that you haven't a chance.

The factors which make for 'feel' when you swing are length and stiffness of the shaft, and the weight of the head. Modern manufacturing techniques are based on a swing weight scale expressed in a letters-and-numbers code. The norm for men's clubs is D2 or D3, and that for

THE DRIVE

Step 21. . . . the right shoulder passes chin and forces head up.

ladies' clubs C8. If these are the clubs you should be using, those with a swing weighting of E3 would feel extremely heavy, and those with C2, impossibly light.

But these ratings are a general guide, and no more. The type of club for each player depends on build, strength, ability, swing speed, experience, how often you play, and a number of other factors. The thing every golfer is looking for is the sensation of swinging the club as fast as possible while feeling in complete control throughout.

Broadly speaking, the less athletic and fit you are, the more flexibility you need in your club. This you will attain with lighter and whippier clubs.

Let us assume that you lead a sedentary life, with your maximum physical activity confined to the opening of the paper on the train in the mornings or the pushing down of clutch, brake and accelerator pedals. The hands will be weak, the figure often portly. For you the swing weighting should be C9 or D1 at the most, and the shaft in the A category; that is, flexible.

For the sportsman from other fields, or those who work manually and are therefore fitter and stronger than the desk-bound brigade, less whip in the shaft will be needed to achieve clubhead speed. For this recruit an R shaft will be advisable, with the normal swing weighting of D0 to D3.

We now move on to the chap who plays regularly, is well built and athletic, and has strong hands. He will use the S (stiff) shaft with a swing weighting in the region of D2 to D5. These ratings will give you an idea of the sort of clubs you need. But in choosing clubs go to the man best able to advise you: your professional.

Grips are made in many colours and of different materials. It is necessary for them to be tacky, for it stands to reason that far more effort is needed to take a firm hold of a leather grip which, through wear, is as shiny as the dining room table.

The most important factor in choosing the grip is to ensure that it is of the right diameter. The normal ones fitted by the manufacturer will suit the average player, but it is obvious

THE DRIVE

Step 22. The hands are high as the end
of the follow-through is near.

that the smaller your hands, the thinner the grip needed, and vice-versa. But remember—change in the thickness of the club will change swing weight.

If you swing clubs with grips too 'fat' for you, you will find it impossible to feel the pressure points (page 54) as you should. I am amazed how few golfers really take trouble over choosing the correct thickness, yet it is one of the most important considerations in setting yourself up with equipment.

How to develop feel

Assuming that you have the right clubs for your physique, fitness, and hands, constant practice will bring that feel without which the good golf shot is impossible. In swinging the club the head should appear at all times to be an extension of the hands, for it is, after all, the head which you are planning to move accurately into the hitting area with the maximum clubhead speed.

With wood shots and the long irons, there is this conscious releasing of the head at the ball. The nearer you get to the green the more delicate will be this relationship between the hands and the blade.

In your warm-up before a game (page 141), give yourself the opportunity of feeling the sweetness of the delicately yet firmly-hit chip and pitch.

Hand and wrist exercises

Henry Cotton is the arch-disciple of hitting with the hands, and throughout his life he has strengthened them by squeezing a squash ball. I have seen him standing talking to a bunch of people in the clubhouse, one hand in his jacket pocket squeezing away at the solid rubber pill.

The wrists can be strengthened by manipulating them in this way, or by using one of those grip expanders you can buy in most sports shops. If you spend a little time each morning getting generally fit, use the time to work with the expanders while running or skipping with an imaginary rope.

Gary Player is, of course, the fitness fanatic supreme. Believing as he does in absolute power, he regularly does fifty press ups on the *fingers*.

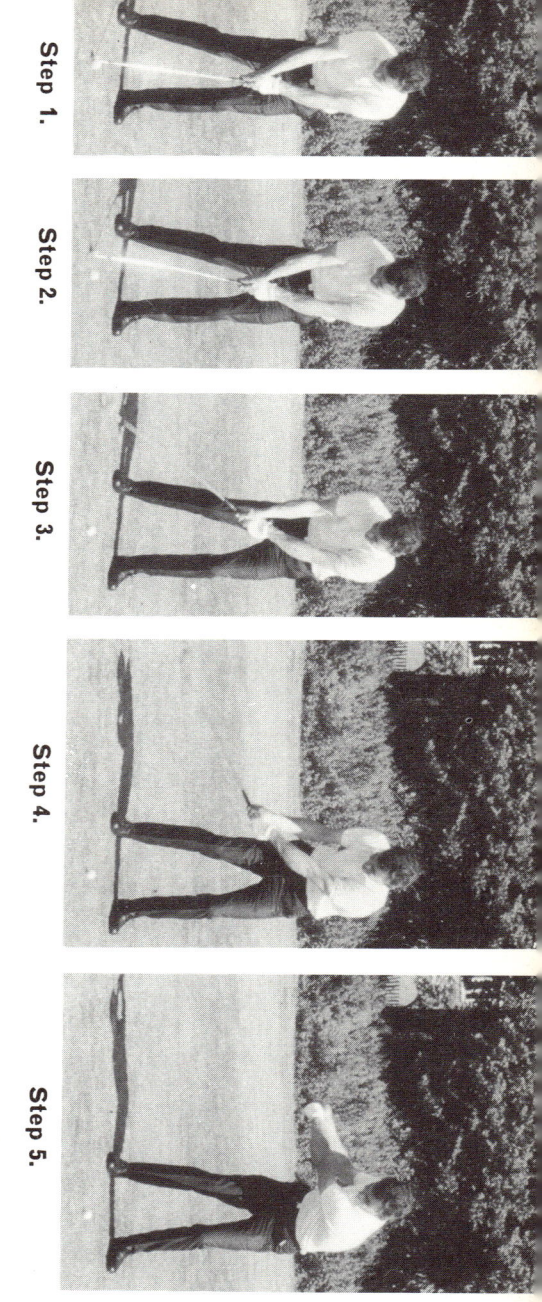

Step 1.

Step 2.

Step 3.

Step 4.

Step 5.

LONG IRON

Steps 1-2-3-4-5. The feet should be placed shoulder width apart with the left foot pointing slightly towards target and the ball round the left instep. Make sure of a smooth takeaway.

Step 9.

Step 8.

Step 7.

Step 6.

Steps 6-7-8-9. At the top of the back swing the hands must be firm. The left hip starts the down swing and generates power like the uncoiling of a spring.

129

Step 10.

Step 11.

Step 12.

Step 13.

Step 14.

LONG IRON

Steps 10-11-12-13-14. On coming into the ball, feel unrestricted, with the club head being released through the ball, not **AT** the ball. Again the head remains perfectly still.

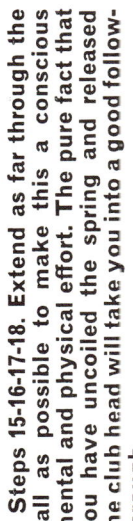

Step 15.    **Step 16.**    **Step 17.**    **Step 18.**

Steps 15-16-17-18. Extend as far through the ball as possible to make this a conscious mental and physical effort. The pure fact that you have uncoiled the spring and released the club head will take you into a good follow-through.

See Flip Sequence of the Long Iron, starting on page 87.

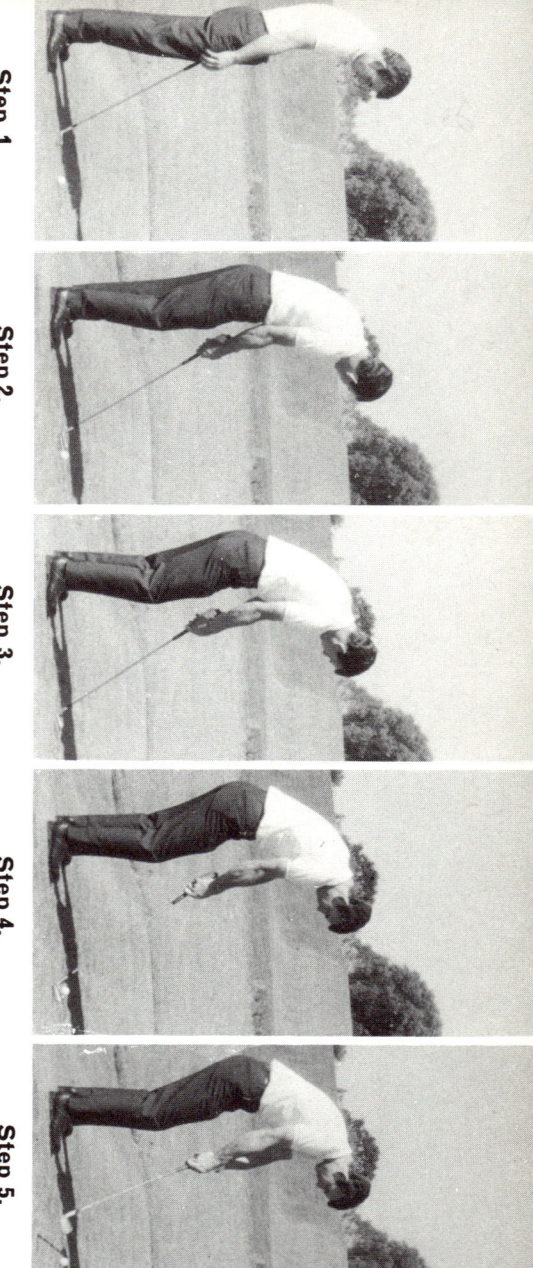

Step 1. **Step 2.** **Step 3.** **Step 4.** **Step 5.**

IRONS FROM THE TEE

Tee up

The one iron has about the same loft as a four wood, but because of the small surface area the strike must be absolutely accurate to get the ball away from the sweet spot. Very few players even take a one iron with them, but with a two or three iron from the tee the ball is naturally teed up lower than for the woods.

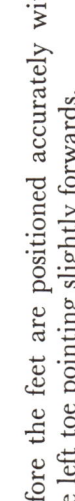

Step 6.    **Step 7.**    **Step 8.**    **Step 9.**

The stance at address for an iron shot from the tee is particularly important, since the target is easily visible and the idea is to get as close to it as possible. The clubface is placed behind the ball and squared up to the target before the feet are positioned accurately with the left toe pointing slightly forwards.

Just because the ball is teed up, there is no excuse for sweeping the ball away. As shown, I have punched down and through the ball,

133

Step 10.

Step 11.

Step 12.

Step 13.

taking a divot after impact. In fact, the shot is identical to that executed from the fairway, and for this reason it is important not to tee the ball too high, as do so many handicap golfers. In

this way, they obviously fail to find the club's sweet spot, losing power because the ball is struck too high up on the blade.

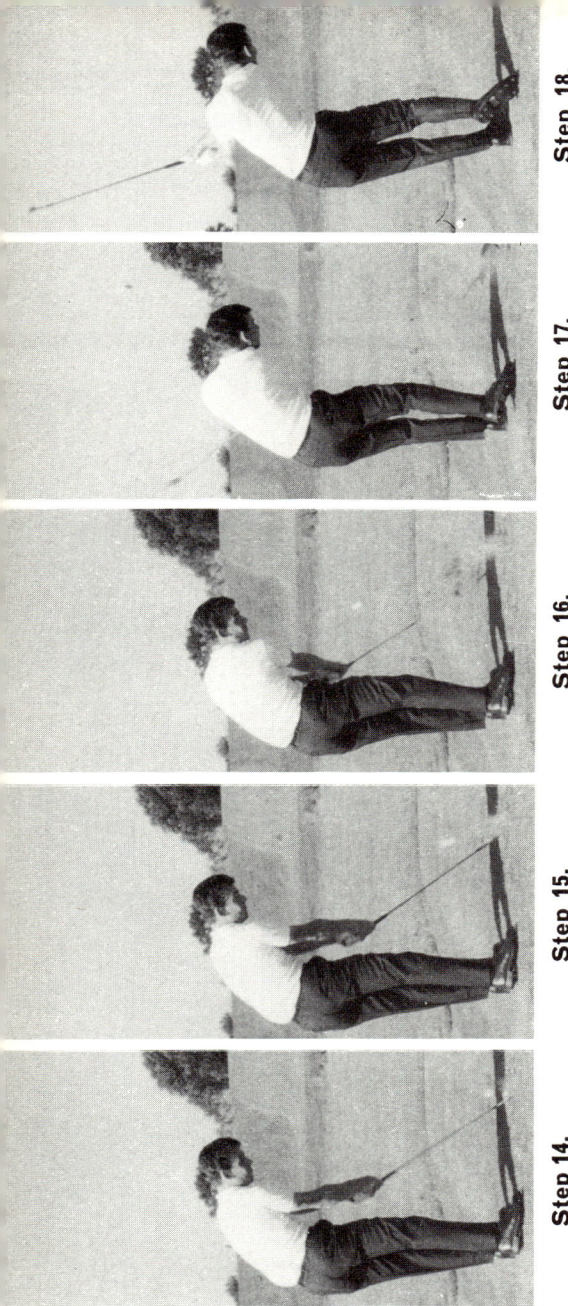

Step 14.   **Step 15.**   **Step 16.**   **Step 17.**   **Step 18.**

Hitting away from hazards

The average golfer will see a hazard on the right of the fairway and place himself on the left hand edge of the tee, fondly believing that from there he will have given himself a few yards' start in avoiding trouble. In fact the opposite is the case. If the trouble is on the right, then tee up near the tee box so that you are in fact hitting away from the hazard. If the traps of other obstacles are on the left of the fairway, tee up on the left hand edge of the teeing ground.

135

OUT OF THE ROUGH

Golf is a game of economy. More unnecessary wastage of strokes occurs in the rough than on the rest of the course put together, and much of this squandering is unnecessary.

Rough comes in all shapes and sizes. But however extensive the area and however deep the grass from which you are trying to escape, your first thought must be to make sure that you are going to get the ball out with your first shot. This brings me to the first axiom in all play from the rough. Never be too ambitious, work out the best route back to the fairway or perhaps on to the green, and make absolutely certain you make your target.

The natural temptation is to go for length. Golfers of all types get a little mad with themselves when they find the rough. The path to disaster is more easily trodden if you go into the wretched stuff with this madness still hanging over you. Invariably take one club higher than your first choice. Only the super-strong can drive the blade of a mid-iron through deep and often clinging grass. Because Arnold Palmer did it at the fifteenth hole at Royal Birkdale during his Open Championship victory there, there is no reason to believe that you can go in for the same sort of heroics. If your first choice of club is, say, a six iron with the green some 150 yards away, take things quietly and step the club up to a seven iron, or maybe an eight or wedge. These clubs may not get you on to the green but they will make absolutely certain that you get clear of the stuff.

With shots from the rough there is always the chance you will get what is known in the profession as a 'flier'. These shots come about when grass is taken through with the club face and is in fact in between the face and the ball. Clearly such a shot will have no vestige of back spin and will career on beyond the green into greenside danger areas. If there is the chance of a flier, club up: that is, use (as is usually advisable in play from the rough) a club which will give you less distance but more certainty of recovering. Never sweep at a ball in the rough. In sweeping, club head speed is not developed to the same extent, the grass over which the sole passes will tie the blade up, and you will be in all sorts of trouble with the force of the shot dissipated before the ball is reached.

If the lie is not too bad, you can often get away with a four wood from what I would call reasonable rough. This club gives you the distance, and many championships have been won by its shrewd use from trouble spots. But the essential is to get back on to the fairway. Boldness is often said to be the golfer's friend, but only fools try to be too bold when in the sort of trouble we are discussing.

In the same area there are those shots from the woods. Never go for a ridiculously narrow gap between the trees. Work out in your own mind which is the best escape route and take it.

At the 18th hole in the Masters at Augusta in 1968 I pushed my drive into the trees between the eighteenth and tenth fairways. Incredibly the lie was a good one, and I had a firing line to the green. I gambled and the gamble came off, but it was not one I would readily take again, or the sort of chance to be even toyed with by the club golfer. If you decide on a safe shot out to the fairway, then use the wedge with a short but unhurried back swing. If you wish to squeeze the ball out low beneath the branches cock the wrists at the start of the back swing with the hands well in front of the ball. To get the ball up quickly, play it off the left toe for what is in effect a flip shot.

THE RIGHT ATTITUDE

The fine limits to which golf has developed at the top have produced an intensive study of the terrain to be attacked and if possible mastered. With so much at stake most great players make an intensive study of the course before beginning a tournament.

Mr. Cliff Roberts, the irascible genius who controls the Masters at Augusta, forbids caddies to go on the course before play, in an effort to ensure that the new pin placings each day are not plotted for the professional players before they go out. I remember his saying to me at the magnificent Augusta National Club: 'The game is becoming tricked up but in my view it should be a test of everything in golf. This business of caddies going out early and reporting back on pin placings is an attempt to cancel out the power of observation which a golfer should possess'.

But at most other tournaments throughout the world you will find caddies on the course long before play begins. For the amateur it would be carrying things a little far to do this before a club match or a game with friends for a few shillings, but there is much you can learn while playing the round.

As you pass greens to be played later make a mental note of where the pin is and of anything else which will aid you when playing the hole.

Golf, as we are so often told, is a matter of playing the percentage shot, and by using your head it is possible to cut two or three strokes off a round. There will be par five holes which you will never hit in two shots. To force a three wood or iron in an attempt to get up in two will make what ought to have been a methodically played par five into a six

ETIQUETTE

Golf is invariably referred to as a gentleman's game. It was at one time also a rich man's game, but now ten million people play it in America and more than a million in Britain.

There is something about golf which brings out the more pleasant side of your character. To go out on a fine bright morning is invariably a happy experience, and if this mood is right, then behaviour will be of the sort associated with golf and golfers.

The joy in golf is to negotiate attractive country in fewer shots than the opposition, and the fun is greater if everyone using the course behaves themselves. The game has a rich tradition of fair-play and courtesy, and it's generally true that the people who play the game do so as a pleasant and rewarding break from the pressures of business, or family life in the case of women. Many clubs now insist on instruction in course etiquette before new

or even seven, and with those figures on your card you will have no chance.

Most amateurs play their golf on one course, and to do this well is a question of using your eyes and head.

The better way into most greens becomes obvious after having played a course a few times, and this is the route the thinking golfer takes. If there is a mid-fairway trap towards the limit of your range with a driver, aim to one side or another if there is enough room, and if not, play short.

If a green is more heavily guarded to the right, make your way in so that the second or third shot can be played without having to negotiate these particular hazards.

Think your way round the course. If, after a poor drive, the chances are against getting up in two, then play the percentage shot which will give you an easy chip or pitch with the chance of a one-putt green for your par.

members are allowed on the course. The natural courtesies make the game more pleasant for all. They embrace consideration for the rights and feelings of others.

Never do anything to disturb the concentration of others. We have all heard of Goldfinger jingling coins in his pocket as James Bond prepared to drive and putt, but this sort of thing should have no place in real life. Never move about or talk when others are preparing to play a shot. Do not stand too close or in any position relative to the opponent which will distract him. Unless you are playing with the sole purpose of instructing someone else, never offer advice, as this is usually a certain way of adding to the poor fellow's troubles. If the other chap is hooking or slicing, let him sort out his own problems or leave them to some time when he can get out with his professional. Play as quickly as possible, and having placed your shot on the tee, do not spend too long admiring it or giving yourself hell if things go wrong. I have played with both amateurs and professionals who expected perfection each time they hit the golf ball, and the game has

been made far less enjoyable by their tantrums and futile self-criticism. On the green, take a reasonable time to get the line of the putt and to prepare for the shot; but do not prowl around as if your life depended on the outcome. Much of the slow play now spreading to Britain in the form of the American five-hour drag is due to the endless antics of players on the green.

If you have lost ground, as defined in the normal rules of etiquette, allow the people behind to come through. Those who hang on like grim death to their position on the course are a menace both to themselves and to those behind them who are out for a few hours relaxation and enjoyment.

To be pressed from behind makes for anxiety, and affects your own shots. It is far better to let those behind through so that you can revert to a normal, sensible pace.

For those who fancy themselves as big hitters, I would say, always have respect for the people in front. Being fired at from very long range by the big bang boys is unnerving if not down-right dangerous.

COMPETING IN A TOURNAMENT

For the professional, each round of a tournament is an event for which he carefully prepares. It appals me that the average club player expects to arrive for a monthly medal or a club match ten minutes before the off, and then to play his best game. So many of them forget that the first few holes are as important as those towards, and at the end of, a round. Three fives on the first three holes could so often be three fours, with maybe a three thrown in, had a player prepared himself properly.

I make it a rule to arrive at the course at least one and a half hours before my tee-off time. I never carry heavy luggage such as a grip or golf bag into the locker room a few minutes before starting time. Most professionals have a caddy to unload their equipment from the car, but if you cannot indulge in this luxury, give your hands time to recover from the effort needed to carry in your gear.

Experiment with this yourself. Dig the garden, carry in your equipment, and go on to the tee. The hands have been used to a far less delicate 'feel' than that of a golf club, and it's ten to one you will make a mess of the shot you play.

This is all part of giving yourself time before a game. Having changed, go to the practice ground and hit some shots. Do not concern yourself particularly with accuracy. Work up to the power you expect to develop when at full stretch with the woods, and then move down to the more accurate playing of the mid-irons and sand wedge. Then go on to the practice green and hit some putts. Again the emphasis should not be on holing every putt but on getting the stroke going and judgement of distance.

If your club has the facilities for you to do this, you will be warmed up in a way which will enable you to start the medal round or the match effectively. Because golf was for long regarded as a leisurely sport, club players have approached it in this way without any thought of a warm-up. But boxers, football players, and athletes get their muscles toned and their eyes in before beginning a match, and a game of golf is as much a test of skill as any other sport. Don't go into a match cold. If your club lacks the facilities for hitting practice balls through the range of woods and irons and for getting the feel of the putter on a practice green, you should play imaginary strokes with all the clubs in the pack.

Go out with the feeling that you have done it all before, and done it as recently as a couple of minutes ago. Sam Snead, one of the greatest competitors of all time, once said: 'To ignore the warm-up is to ignore the very existence of both the golf swing and the problems of the game'. The fellow who steps straight from his car into the locker room and then on to the tee believing that he can master golf's problems is the sort of fellow you should play regularly for money.

INDEX